Hurricane Katrina

PETER BENOIT

Children's Press®
An Imprint of Scholastic Inc.
New York Toronto London Auckland Sydney
Mexico City New Delhi Hong Kong
Danbury, Connecticut

Content Consultant

Jack Williams

Founding editor of the *USA Today* weather page and author of *The AMS Weather Book: The Ultimate Guide to America's Weather*

Library of Congress Cataloging-in-Publication Data

Hurricane Katrina / Peter Benoit.
    p. cm.—(A true book)
Includes bibliographical references and index.
ISBN-13: 978-0-531-25421-9 (lib. bdg.)   ISBN-13: 978-0-531-26626-7 (pbk.)
ISBN-10: 0-531-25421-6 (lib. bdg.)   ISBN-10: 0-531-26626-5 (pbk.)
    1. Hurricane Katrina, 2005—Juvenile literature. 2. Hurricanes—Social aspects—Louisiana—New Orleans—Juvenile literature. 3. Disaster relief—Louisiana—New Orleans—Juvenile literature.
I. Title. II. Series.
    HV636 2005 .L8 B46 2011
    976.3'35064—dc22   2011007145

Find the Truth!

Everything you are about to read is true *except* for one of the sentences on this page.

Which one is **TRUE**?

T or F No levees broke in New Orleans.

T or F No future hurricanes will be named Katrina.

Find the answers in this book.

Contents

THE BIG TRUTH!

Where Else Did Katrina Hit?

Vice Admiral Thad Allen with President George W. Bush

Experts warn people to leave potential flood zones before a hurricane hits.

This satellite image shows Katrina over the Gulf of Mexico. The red dotted line shows the hurricane's path.

MISSISSIPPI ALABAMA

LOUISIANA

Mobile

Biloxi

FLORIDA

New Orleans

Gulf of Mexico

Areas hit hard by Katrina

0   50 MI

Mobile

New Orleans   Biloxi

Miami

The National Hurricane Center, which tracks storms and hurricanes with satellite images like this one, never closes.

CHAPTER 1

Hurricane Coming!

One of the most destructive hurricanes in U.S. history first appeared on **satellite images** on August 24, 2005. A **tropical storm** was forming over the Bahamas. The National **Hurricane** Center named it Katrina. It became a hurricane the next day, when its winds reached 74 miles per hour. It hit Florida two hours later.

The National Hurricane Center in Miami had forecast the storm's path. Florida governor Jeb Bush had already declared a state of emergency. Public schools closed. Shelters opened for people who were unsafe at home.

Category One in Florida

Winds were blowing 80 miles (129 kilometers) per hour. Katrina was now a Category One hurricane, the weakest type of hurricane. Still, it dumped more than 1 foot (30 centimeters) of rain in some places. Enough water fell to cause flooding. High winds and falling trees brought down power lines. Hurricane Katrina spent seven hours over Florida. It resulted in the deaths of fourteen people and almost $2 billion in damage.

Heavy rains and flooding made travel nearly impossible in Florida.

Katrina was the first hurricane to directly hit the National Hurricane Center offices in Miami since 1964.

Measuring Hurricanes

Wind **engineer** Herb Saffir and **meteorologist** Bob Simpson originally developed the Saffir-Simpson Hurricane Wind Scale. This tool helps people plan for possible hurricanes.

Category	Wind Speed	Expected Damage
1	74–95 miles (119–153 km) per hour	Some
2	96–110 miles (155–177 km) per hour	Extensive
3	111–130 miles (179–209 km) per hour	Devastating
4	131–155 miles (211–249 km) per hour	Catastrophic
5	Greater than 155 miles (250 km) per hour	Catastrophic

Monster Storm

The energy provided by warm water strengthens hurricanes. Hurricane Katrina crossed an unusually warm ocean **current** as it moved west. This current increased the wind speed. On August 27, Katrina became a Category Three hurricane. Katrina doubled in size over the next day. Its winds were blowing more than 175 miles (280 km) per hour. The massive hurricane was now a Category Five as it moved northwest toward states bordering the Gulf of Mexico—Louisiana, Mississippi, and Alabama.

Areas along the Gulf Coast were already flooding before Katrina hit.

The Atlantic storm season had a record 15 hurricanes in 2005.

New Orleans mayor Ray Nagin held a press conference warning the citizens to head for higher ground.

Moving Out of the Storm's Path

On August 27, President George W. Bush declared a state of emergency for the areas in the storm's path. Officials across southern Louisiana asked or ordered people to leave. New Orleans Mayor Ray Nagin only suggested that city residents **evacuate**. He warned, "We're facing the storm most of us have feared."

Highways leading out of New Orleans were clogged with heavy traffic.

Leaving New Orleans

The National Hurricane Center predicted Katrina would make **landfall** near New Orleans. Mayor Nagin ordered everyone to leave the city. Officials used school buses to evacuate residents. But there were not enough drivers. Four out of five residents left. Many who remained were too poor, old, or ill to leave. As Katrina's rains began to fall, thousands of people realized they could not escape.

Built in a Bowl

New Orleans was surrounded by water. Parts of the city were originally built on drained swamp land. Canals, pumps, flood walls, and earthen slopes called **levees** were supposed to keep the city from flooding. They formed a sort of bowl with New Orleans at the bottom. The bottom of the bowl would flood if water broke through the levees. The city's rich history was in danger of being destroyed.

It didn't take long for Katrina's drenching rains to flood the streets of New Orleans.

As Katrina came ashore, rainfall exceeded 1 inch (2.5 centimeters) per hour. ➡️

Boats and large ships were flung onto shore by winds and flooding near Buras, Louisiana.

CHAPTER 2

Devastation

Katrina weakened to a very strong Category Three storm after midnight on August 29. Offshore waves were as high as four-story buildings. Winds as fast as 130 miles (209 km) per hour howled. Heavy rain had already filled the four major canals that drained New Orleans. At 6:10 a.m., Katrina made landfall about 65 miles south of New Orleans. By then, Katrina spanned more than 400 miles (640 km).

← Hurricanes are most likely in the Atlantic Ocean, Carribbean Sea, and Gulf of Mexico from June 1 to November 30.

Storm Surge

One of the most devastating parts of a hurricane is the **storm surge**. A storm surge is the wall of wind-driven water that comes before a hurricane. Storm surges as high as 19 feet (5.79 meters) washed into New Orleans. Katrina's storm surge peaked at 27.8 feet (8.5 m) in Pass Christian, Mississippi. It was the highest surge ever recorded on a U.S. coastline. The water ran inland 6 miles (10 km). It carried boats, barges, and oil rigs. It washed away buildings and bridges.

All that was left of Pass Christian's middle school after Katrina was a pile of rubble.

By August 31, more than 80 percent of New Orleans was under floodwater.

Water quickly flooded through the broken levees.

Danger in New Orleans

Just southeast of New Orleans, the surge and heavy rainfall overwhelmed local levees. Water quickly rose above house roofs. High winds blew out windows, tore trees out of the ground by the roots, and flattened houses. At about 9 a.m., holes called **breaches** opened in the levees alongside the 17th Street Canal. The London Avenue Canal levees simply blew apart. About 8 feet (2.4 m) of water poured into New Orleans.

Katrina brought far too much water for the floodwalls to handle.

A City Underwater

Concrete and steel walls built on top of levees to stop floodwaters are called **floodwalls**. Throughout the morning, breaches appeared in the floodwalls along the Industrial Canal. Water rushed into the city's Lower Ninth Ward, one of the city's poorest neighborhoods. The city pumps could not drain away the water fast enough. Wind also damaged some of the buildings that housed the pumps.

Rising water soon turned the Lower Ninth Ward and part of the east side into a lake. By evening, at least two-thirds of New Orleans was underwater.

More Breaches

August 30 dawned with rescue workers in no better position than the residents. Some police officers and firefighters found boats to rescue the tens of thousands of people stranded on the upper floors of buildings. Dozens of others waited on the Fillmore Bridge. They were cut off in both directions by water. Neighborhoods that had been dry the previous day began to fill with water. In time, more than 50 breaches in the levees and floodwalls occurred.

This satellite image shows the approximate depth of floodwaters in New Orleans on August, 31, 2005.

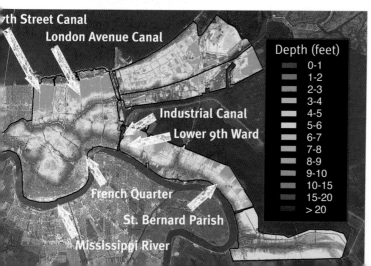

th Street Canal
London Avenue Canal

Depth (feet)
0-1
1-2
2-3
3-4
4-5
5-6
6-7
7-8
8-9
9-10
10-15
15-20
> 20

Industrial Canal
Lower 9th Ward

French Quarter
St. Bernard Parish
Mississippi River

The most deadly U.S. hurricane, which hit Galveston, Texas, in 1900, took about 8,000 lives.

Katrina Moves Inland

Katrina battered towns along Mississippi's coast as it pulled north. Coming ashore at high tide raised the surge and waves even higher. Neighborhoods and towns near coastal beaches were wiped out. Barges ended up hundreds of yards from the coast. Waves dropped boats onto houses.

Heavy objects, such as this boat, often ended up far from their original locations after Katrina passed through.

In Mississippi, 11 tornadoes spun off from Katrina.

Airboats were used to evacuate people from Memorial Medical Center.

Waiting for Help

Memorial Medical Center in New Orleans was located 3 feet (1 m) below sea level. The hospital had water 10 feet (3 m) deep on its ground floor. Electricity was out. There were no working elevators. Staff members had to carry patients up flights of stairs. Temperatures inside soared to 100 degrees Fahrenheit (38 degrees Celsius). Desperate doctors and nurses wondered where help was. Some 80,000 others stranded in the city also wondered when they would be rescued. So did television viewers around the world watching the disaster.

Where Else Did Katrina Hit?

Most news coverage of Katrina focused on the hurricane's effect on New Orleans. But Katrina also had a huge impact on other parts of the southeastern United States. Homes and businesses were destroyed as the hurricane hit towns and cities all along the Gulf Coast. New Orleans drew the most attention, but people in other parts of Louisiana, as well as in Mississippi, Alabama, and parts of Florida had just as much destruction to deal with.

Florida

Katrina first came ashore on the evening of August 25. It hit the beaches of Florida's southeastern coast. Winds blew at 80 miles (129 km) per hour, knocking down trees and killing at least two people.

Biloxi and Gulfport, Mississippi

On August 29, the hurricane's strongest winds slammed into coastal Mississippi. It hit Biloxi, Gulfport, and other smaller towns in the area. Most buildings in the towns were damaged. Many were destroyed. Almost all businesses were shut down, leaving many people out of work. Phone lines and cell towers were also ruined. People were unable to communicate.

Mobile, Alabama

Cities such as Mobile, Alabama, were affected by Katrina's outer edges. The damage was not as extensive as in Biloxi or New Orleans. Downtown Mobile was under several feet of floodwater. Winds of 80 miles (129 kph) per hour hit the city, causing structural damage.

With their homes underwater or destroyed, tens of thousands of people were trapped in the Superdome with nowhere to go.

The Situation at the Superdome

On the morning of August 31, more than 25,000 people with nowhere to go had taken shelter at the Louisiana Superdome in New Orleans. Rain poured in through holes that the wind had blown in the roof. Toilet paper, clean water, and medical supplies were gone. At least six people died at the Superdome.

After Katrina, the Louisiana Superdome was closed for 13 months. The repairs cost almost $200 million.

Leadership Problems

Many people felt that government officials showed a lack of leadership during the disaster. Officials did not prepare residents effectively or evacuate them efficiently. The U.S. government's Federal Emergency Management Agency (FEMA) failed to organize rescue efforts successfully. Many blamed all levels of government for the weak response to the disaster.

President George W. Bush (second from left) and New Orleans mayor Ray Nagin (second from right) were among the leaders blamed for the poor handling of the disaster.

FEMA director Michael Brown failed to provide the leadership required for a catastrophe as immense as Hurricane Katrina.

Disaster Response

Government officials were unsuccessful in rescue efforts. FEMA director Michael Brown always seemed hours or days behind the events shown on television. FEMA turned down offers of equipment, airplanes, and supplies from other states and nations. President Bush told Brown, "You're doing a heck of a job, Brownie." Criticism of the failures grew louder after this remark.

Local Heroes

Louisiana governor Kathleen Blanco ordered the Louisiana Department of Wildlife and Fisheries (LDWF) to help with rescues. LDWF took over a waterlogged bridge and made it their headquarters. The agency used its many boats to pull people out of damaged houses and a local hospital. In six days, they rescued more than 10,000 people in the city and nearby areas.

The LDWF helped bring thousands of people to safety after Katrina.

People who fled Katrina ended up living in all 50 states.

Thousands of people were bused from New Orleans to the Astrodome in Houston, Texas.

Where to Go

On September 1, the situation remained serious. Buses took about 5,000 people to the Astrodome in Houston, Texas. They found only 2,000 cots waiting for them.

Thousands of people in New Orleans tried to cross a bridge to the town of Gretna. But Gretna police officers barred their way with guns. Gretna's police chief later said his town had no food or shelter to offer.

Large trailer parks were created to hold the thousands of trailers that became home for many hurricane victims.

Help at Last

FEMA started to catch up in September. It moved trailers into the area to serve as housing. The 700,000 requests for help swamped the effort. Some did not want to leave the area. They stayed in hotel rooms paid for by FEMA. Other people left for places all over the country.

Help From Around the World

Other organizations and government agencies began to arrive. The U.S. Coast Guard rescued 30,000 people affected by the hurricane. The American Red Cross and the Salvation Army provided food and shelter to victims. People from around the world sent food, blankets, and bottled water. More than 70 countries offered help. Some donated money to the relief efforts. Others sent ships and water pumps.

Aid organizations provided bottled water and other necessities to hurricane victims.

Kuwait made the largest single donation to the Katrina recovery efforts — $500 million.

Rescue boats provided the main method of rescue for stranded New Orleans residents.

Other Offers of Help

Individuals also came to help after Katrina. On September 2, more than 1,000 firefighters met in Atlanta, Georgia, with plans to travel to New Orleans as soon as possible. Some people took their own boats and headed for the city. Professional divers helped with search and rescue missions.

Violence and Anger

The Katrina disaster led to crime in some places. People trapped in New Orleans without food or clean water sometimes took what they needed from stores. Violent crimes such as murder, robbery, and car theft were committed. In a few cases, frustration with the relief effort led to gunfire between residents and police. People everywhere searched for someone to blame.

A woman looks into what is left of a drugstore after looters broke in following Katrina.

After Katrina, one-third of the New Orleans police deserted the city. ➡

Volunteers have helped to rebuild New Orleans and surrounding communities since the destruction of 2005.

CHAPTER 4

Rebuilding New Orleans

The official death count from Hurricane Katrina and the resulting floods reached 1,836. An estimated $81 billion in damage makes it the most expensive natural disaster in U.S. history. With such extensive destruction, rebuilding New Orleans has proven to be a long and difficult task.

In 2005, the World Meteorological Organization removed the name Katrina from its list of hurricane names, as it does for most deadly storms.

The Path to Reconstruction

Putting New Orleans back together again was a long process. It took six months to restore electricity in some places. Flood waters remained in low-lying neighborhoods for weeks. Power and water returned slowly. In 2010, the city had an estimated 363,000 residents. But many people had difficulty finding homes when they returned.

Some New Orleans residents did not return to their homes for months or even years.

The French Quarter is the oldest neighborhood in New Orleans.

Many in the French Quarter were able to begin cleanup efforts within days of the storm.

Most of the damage to New Orleans' buildings didn't come from the hurricane winds. It came from the floods that occurred when the levees failed. Neighborhoods built on higher ground, such as the historic French Quarter, had much less damage than lower parts of the city. Rebuilding has been much easier and quicker in these areas.

In 2007, New Orleans sued the Army Corps of Engineers for $77 billion.

Levees and floodwalls were rebuilt using designs to prevent a disaster such as the flooding from Katrina from happening again.

Getting Rid of the Water

One of the first things that needed to be done was to drain the floodwaters and repair the levees. The powerful waters had broken through the levees in 53 places. These holes had to be fixed before the next year's hurricane season. The levees also needed to be stronger than they had been before. The U.S. Army Corps of Engineers worked quickly to fix all the breaks.

Pointing Fingers

Many people blamed the government's slow response and lack of leadership for the damage that occurred in New Orleans. They also questioned the design and construction of the levees. Some people believed that support posts had not been installed deep enough into the ground. This placed some of the blame on the U.S. Army Corps of Engineers and the companies that had built the levees.

Several government panels have attempted to address the problems of the levees in New Orleans.

Building New Homes

Katrina left hundreds of thousands of people homeless. Volunteers and charitable organizations worked together to help build new homes for the hurricane victims. Volunteers from around the country worked with Habitat for Humanity to build hundreds of new houses. Actor Brad Pitt started the Make It Right program to build 150 environmentally friendly homes in the Lower Ninth Ward neighborhood.

Timeline of Hurricane Katrina

August 25

Katrina develops into a Category One hurricane and hits southern Florida.

August 29

Katrina makes landfall on the Gulf Coast.

Tourism Returns

Katrina had destroyed New Orleans' thriving tourism business. As the industry began to recover, it brought money and support to the city from all around the world. In June 2006, the American Library Association held its annual conference in the recovering city. The event drew thousands of people. It also encouraged other organizations to hold conventions in New Orleans. People also began vacationing in New Orleans once again.

September 1
Officials begin evacuating thousands from the Louisiana Superdome.

September 8
The U.S. Congress approves almost $52 billion for relief efforts.

Hope for the Future

Many of New Orleans' neighborhoods have recovered in the years following Katrina. Others are still rebuilding. More and more progress is made every day. By 2010, almost 90 percent of New Orleans' population and 70 percent of its jobs had returned. The U.S. government has promised to invest billions of dollars more in the coming years. The city is on its way to an incredible recovery. ★

New Orleans' famous music scene has also returned since Katrina.

True Statistics

Speed of Hurricane Katrina's maximum winds: More than 175 mi. (280 km) per hour

Width of Katrina at landfall: More than 400 mi. (644 km)

Peak storm surge: 27.8 ft. (8.5 m)

Amount of New Orleans underwater on August 29: At least two-thirds

Number of countries offering help: More than 70

Number of deaths caused by Katrina: 1,836

Estimated total cost of storm damage: $81 billion

Number of refugees in Superdome: About 25,000

Did you find the truth?

(F) No levees broke in New Orleans.

(T) No future hurricanes will be named Katrina.

Resources

Books

Carson, Mary Kay. *Inside Hurricanes*. New York: Sterling, 2010.

Fine, Jil. *Floods*. New York: Children's Press, 2007.

Fradin, Judith B., and Dennis B. Fradin. *Hurricane Katrina*. New York: Benchmark, 2009.

Hoffman, Mary Ann. *Hurricane Katrina*. New York: PowerKids, 2006.

Miller, Mara. *Hurricane Katrina Strikes the Gulf Coast*. Berkeley Heights, NJ: Enslow, 2006.

Royston, Angela. *Hurricanes*. New York: Franklin Watts, 2011.

Strom, Laura Layton. *Built Below Sea Level: New Orleans*. New York: Children's Press, 2007.

Torres, John A. *Hurricane Katrina and the Devastation of New Orleans, 2005*. Hockessin, DE: Mitchell Lane, 2006.

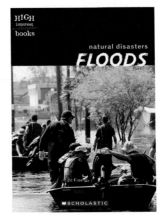

Organizations and Web Sites

Katrina: Though the Eyes of Children

www.katrinaexhibit.org/photoalbum/index.htm

Look at artwork created by children forced from their homes by Katrina.

New Orleans Times-Picayune: Hurricane Katrina

www.nola.com/katrina

Study a huge archive of stories, photos, videos, and other materials on Katrina collected by the New Orleans newspaper.

Places to Visit

Louisiana State Museum

751 Chartres Street
New Orleans, LA 70116
(504) 568-6968
http://lsm.crt.state.la.us
See videos and photographs from during and after the disaster at the museum's exhibit "Living With Hurricanes: Katrina and Beyond."

Smithsonian National Museum of American History

14th Street and Constitution Avenue NW
Washington, DC 20013-7012
(202) 633-1000
http://americanhistory.si.edu
Visit an exhibit of objects collected from areas affected by Katrina.

Important Words

breaches (BREECH-ez)—holes in a wall or levee

current (KUR-uhnt)—a movement of water in a certain direction

engineer (ehn-juh-NIHR)—someone who is trained to design and build structures, machines, and systems

evacuate (i-VAK-yoo-ate)—to get away from a dangerous area

floodwalls (FLUHD-wallz)—concrete or steel walls built on top of levees to stop floodwaters

landfall (LAND-fall)— the point at which a hurricane's center, called the eye, hits land

hurricane (HER-uh-kane) a storm formed over warm water with winds of at least 74 miles (119 km) per hour

levees (LEV-eez)—walls of dirt or other material built to stop flooding

meteorologist (mee-tee-ur-OL-oh-jist)—someone who studies Earth's atmosphere and weather

satellite images (SAT-uh-lite IM-ih-jez)—pictures taken from an object launched to orbit Earth

storm surge (STORM SURJ)—the wall of wind-driven water that comes before a hurricane

tropical storm (TROP-uh-kuhl STORM)—a storm formed over warm water with winds between 39 miles (63 km) per hour and 73 mph (117 kph)

Index

Page numbers in **bold** indicate illustrations

About the Author

Peter Benoit is educated as a mathematician but has many other interests. He has taught and tutored high school and college students for many years, mostly in math and science. He also runs summer workshops for writers and students of literature. Mr. Benoit has written more than 2,000 poems. His life has been one committed to learning. He lives in Greenwich, New York.